PETE WILSON

BIBLE STUDY

WHAT KEEPS YOU UP AT

NIGHT?

HOW TO FIND
PEACE WHILE CHASING
YOUR DREAMS

LifeWay Press®
Nashville, Tennessee

Published by LifeWay Press® · © 2015 Pete Wilson

ISBN 978-1-4300-4245-7 · Item 005747963
Dewey decimal classification: 152.4 · Subject headings: FEAR \ ANXIETY \ FAITH

To order additional copies of this resource, write to LifeWay Church Resources Customer Service; One LifeWay Plaza; Nashville, TN 37234-0113; fax 615.251.5933; phone toll free 800.458.2772; order online at *www.lifeway.com;* email *orderentry@ lifeway.com;* or visit the LifeWay Christian Store serving you.

Printed in the United States of America

Groups Ministry Publishing · LifeWay Resources
One LifeWay Plaza · Nashville, TN 37234-0152

CONTENTS

THE AUTHOR

Pete Wilson is the founding and senior pastor of Cross Point Church in Nashville, Tennessee, a committed church community that he and his wife, Brandi, planted in 2002. Cross Point has grown to reach more than five thousand people each weekend through its five campuses located around the Nashville area and online.

Cross Point is an outreach ministry focused on helping people become devoted to Christ, irrevocably committed to one another, and relentlessly dedicated to reaching those outside God's family with the gospel. As one of the fastest-growing churches in America, the ministry has made Pete a frequent speaker at national and international church conferences. He gained national attention in 2010 with his best-selling book, *Plan B*.

Pete is an avid blogger *(www.PeteWilson.tv)*. He also enjoys the outdoors, farming, and Titans football. When he's looking for rest, you can often find Pete working in his garden, hanging out with Brandi, or playing outside with their three sons.

ABOUT THIS STUDY

Everyone deals with fear. For some of us, fear can become paralyzing. But what if the real problem isn't an overwhelming fear but an underwhelming faith?

My prayer is that over the course of this study, you'll take steps of trust on the path toward God's best for your life; that you'll be granted faith to face the fear that will try to blockade you; that you'll step out of the boat and start walking toward Jesus; and that He will bring into your life the people, resources, and circumstances that will enable you to withstand doubt, opposition, and worry.

HOW TO GET THE MOST FROM THIS STUDY

ATTEND EACH GROUP EXPERIENCE.
- Watch the video teaching.

- Participate in the group discussions.

COMPLETE THE MATERIAL IN THIS BIBLE STUDY BOOK.
Take one step at a time. Each session provides material for group discussion based on the video teaching (organized as Start, Watch, and Respond) and for personal study between sessions (organized as Personal Reflection, Deeper Look, and Now What?) You may want to spread out the personal study by doing one section every other day. Related Scriptures are provided if you'd like something to read each day of the week.

Be honest with yourself and others about your fears, your questions, and your experiences as you study and apply the material.

Ask God to show you His truth about each topic so that you can overcome your fears and embrace the great adventure He's planned for your life.

OBTAIN AND READ PETE WILSON'S BOOK
WHAT KEEPS YOU UP AT NIGHT?
Thomas Nelson, 2015, ISBN 978-0-8499-6457-2

TIPS FOR LEADING A SMALL GROUP

PRAYERFULLY PREPARE

Prepare for each meeting by reviewing the weekly material and group questions ahead of time and praying for each person in the group. Ask the Holy Spirit to work through you and the group discussion as you point to Jesus each week through God's Word.

MINIMIZE DISTRACTIONS

Create a comfortable environment. If group members are uncomfortable, they'll be distracted and therefore not engaged in the group experience. Plan ahead by taking into consideration seating, temperature, lighting, food or drink, surrounding noise, and general cleanliness (put away pets if meeting in a home).

At best, thoughtfulness and hospitality show guests and group members they're welcome and valued in whatever environment you choose to gather. At worst, people may never notice your effort, but they're also not distracted. Do everything in your ability to help people focus on what's most important: connecting with God, with the Bible, and with others.

INCLUDE OTHERS

Your goal is to foster a community in which people are welcome just as they are but encouraged to grow spiritually. Always be aware of opportunities to—

- **INVITE** new people to join your group;

- **INCLUDE** any people who visit the group.

An inexpensive way to make first-time guests feel welcome or to invite someone to get involved is to give them their own copies of this Bible study book.

ENCOURAGE DISCUSSION

A good small group experience has the following characteristics.

EVERYONE PARTICIPATES. Encourage everyone to ask questions, share responses, or read aloud.

NO ONE DOMINATES—NOT EVEN THE LEADER. Be sure your time speaking as a leader takes up less than half of your time together as a group. Politely guide discussion if anyone dominates.

NOBODY IS RUSHED THROUGH QUESTIONS. Don't feel that a moment of silence is a bad thing. People often need time to think about their responses to questions they've just heard or to gain courage to share what God is stirring in their hearts.

INPUT IS AFFIRMED AND FOLLOWED UP. Make sure you point out something true or helpful in a response. Don't just move on. Build community with follow-up questions, asking how other people have experienced similar things or how a truth has shaped their understanding of God and the Scripture you're studying. People are less likely to speak up if they fear that you don't actually want to hear their answers or that you're looking for only a certain answer.

GOD AND HIS WORD ARE CENTRAL. Opinions and experiences can be helpful, but God has given us the truth. Trust Scripture to be the authority and God's Spirit to work in people's lives. You can't change anyone, but God can. Continually point people to the Word and to active steps of faith.

KEEP CONNECTING

Think of ways to connect with group members during the week. Participation during the group session is always improved when members spend time connecting with one another outside the group sessions. The more people are comfortable with and involved in one another's lives, the more they'll look forward to being together. When people move beyond being friendly to truly being friends who form a community, they come to each session eager to engage instead of merely attending.

Encourage group members with thoughts, commitments, or questions from the session by connecting through emails, texts, and social media.

When possible, build deeper friendships by planning or spontaneously inviting group members to join you outside your regularly scheduled group time for meals; fun activities; and projects around your home, church, or community.

WEEK ONE
REDEFINING FEAR

START

Welcome to our first session of *What Keeps You Up at Night?*

- What do you do when you're having trouble sleeping at night? Count sheep? Walk around? Eat? Read? Watch TV? Something else?

- What do you hope to get from a study called *What Keeps You Up at Night?*

As we'll see, every one of us has fears in our lives, fears that can keep us up at night, paralyze us, and keep us from becoming all God wants us to be. In this Bible study we'll look at these fears; the effects they have on us; ways people in the Bible faced their fears; and why we can ruthlessly trust God's plan, even in the face of difficulties and uncertainty. Each week we'll identify ways to come to grips with our fears and ways we can trust God in the midst of them.

Let's see what Pete has to say in the first video session about our fears.

WATCH

Use the space below to follow along and take notes as you watch video session 1.

Fear is a thief.

Everyone has something that they fear
Keeps us from becoming the person God wants us to be
Erases my faith
Takes the steps forward even when we are afraid
God helps us with our fear
Fear not, Don't be afraid

Fear: a heightened sense of vulnerability and a diminished sense of power

Combat fear with faith. Genesis 39:2
Trust God more.
Focus my attention on God
God always has a plan for good
God controls everything

You always combat fear with faith.

The goal is not to fear less but to trust God more.

Scriptures: Matthew 9:2,22; 10:31; Mark 5:36; Luke 5:10; 8:50; 12:4,32; John 6:20; Genesis 37:24; 39:2,13-21; 40:14,23; 41:9-13; 50:19-20

Video sessions available for purchase
at *www.lifeway.com/upatnight*

RESPOND

Use the statements and questions below to discuss the video.

Pete identified some of the things he fears most in life, things like blowing an important decision or failing to be the husband and father God wants him to be. So let's begin by responding to his question:

What are a couple of things in life that you fear most?

Pete defined *fear* as *a heightened sense of vulnerability and a diminished sense of power.*

Have you ever thought of fear this way?

In what ways is this definition helpful?

Pete said, "Scripture tells us that if you have fear in your life—and we all do—it's not that you have a fear problem; it's that you have a faith problem. The goal is not to live a fear-free life. Our goal is to learn to trust God more."

How did you feel about that statement? Why?

How does it make you feel to know that Jesus cares about your fears, so much so that he often encouraged us, "Do not be afraid," "Have courage," or "Take heart"?

The recurring pattern of Joseph's life involved going from one dire situation to another. Yet Scripture repeatedly says the Lord was with Joseph, and he prospered.

In what ways can you personally relate to Joseph's experiences?

Where are you right now in your life? In the bottom of a figurative cistern or jail cell, in the palace, or somewhere in between?

Pete stressed that instead of focusing on his problems and fears, Joseph focused on God. One example is after Joseph was falsely accused and then thrown into an Egyptian prison. The Bible says:

> The LORD was with Joseph and extended kindness to him. He granted him favor in the eyes of the prison warden. The warden did not bother with anything under Joseph's authority, because the LORD was with him, and the LORD made everything that he did successful.
> **GENESIS 39:21,23**

What did you learn from Joseph about keeping your focus on God even in the midst of difficult situations?

Finally, Joseph was able to look back over all his circumstances and see what God was doing all along. He told his brothers:

> You planned evil against me; God planned it for good.
> **GENESIS 50:20**

Pete made the point that clarity often comes only in hindsight.

As you look back over situations in your past, how do you now see God's involvement that you didn't see at the time?

How does that insight help you trust God today?

This week watch for situations in which you might normally tend to focus your attention on your problems and fears. Notice when you begin to feel that way. What are you doing? Where are you at the time? Whom are you with, or are you alone? What prompts you to begin to feel fear—a heightened sense of vulnerability and a diminished sense of power? Intentionally notice of where that fear comes from. Then try to hold on to Jesus' words: "Have courage." "Take heart." "Do not be afraid."

Complete the personal study for week 1 before the next group experience.

FEAR WILL KEEP YOU FROM BECOMING THE PERSON GOD CREATED YOU TO BECOME.

PERSONAL REFLECTION

We must start this time of personal reflection by simply acknowledging, "I fear." We all fear. And we should also recognize right up front that this fear is a dirty enemy; it doesn't fight fair. It finds our soft spots, our weak links, and mercilessly exploits them. It whispers lies in our ears at night and saps our strength in the morning.

Even for mighty King David—"a man after [God's] own heart" (1 Sam. 13:14, NASB), the same guy who as a boy slew Goliath, the warrior-king who had unbridled trust and confidence in God—the natural reaction was to feel fear in the midst of overwhelming circumstances. On one such occasion he wrote:

> My heart shudders within me;
> terrors of death sweep over me.
> Fear and trembling grip me;
> horror has overwhelmed me.
> I said, "If only I had wings like a dove!
> I would fly away and find rest.
> How far away I would flee;
> I would stay in the wilderness."
> **PSALM 55:4-7**

So what keeps you up at night? In the group session you were asked to share one of your fears. Perhaps that took courage for you to admit a particular fear publicly. Now think about any fears that are more difficult for you to talk about openly.

List five or six of your worst fears—things that have the power to rob your life of joy, happiness, and hope.

What's your biggest fear? Circle it or add it to your list.

Select the consequences of fear that affect you most seriously.

☐ Fear steals my joy in the present and robs me of my hope
for the future.
☐ Fear causes me to obsess on myself and my limitations
instead of seeing all the possibilities that are available.
☐ Fear keeps me from connecting with other people.
☐ Fear prevents me from allowing myself to trust.
☐ Fear erodes my faith and confidence, preventing me from
daring to do what God has called me to do.
☐ Fear paralyzes me; it keeps me from letting go of the things
that feel secure in my life in order to reach out and take risks.
☐ Fear deceives me into seeking safety when I was actually
created to embrace life as an adventure.
☐ Fear causes my vision to get skewed by my circumstances,
and I start to see things inaccurately. Often I see things
that don't even exist!
☐ Fear disorients me. It causes me to fight nonexistent enemies;
it causes me to focus on the wrong things.

Identify a recent example of at least one of these consequences of fear.

When you consider your fears and their consequences in your life,
where are you focusing your attention—on the fears or on God?
Circle the number on the scale below that reflects your current focus.

1	2	3	4	5	6	7	8	9	10
Fear/problems/consequences									God

Why did you assign yourself that score?

Wherever you happen to be on this scale at the moment, give yourself some grace. The important thing at this point is to simply know where you are and to make an honest assessment of your current condition.

When do you most often sense fear in your life? Identify specific situations. For instance, are you with people or alone? Do certain people or situations trigger this fear?

Your fears are real; there's no doubt about that. But know that your worries and fears don't have to keep you from moving forward. The important thing isn't that you fear something; it's that you have a God bigger than anything you fear.

OPEN YOUR BIBLE AND HIGHLIGHT PSALM 23:4.

With your Bible still open to Psalm 23, take a few moments to pray as this verse prompts you. Tell God, your Shepherd, that even though you're walking through this dark valley, you'll turn these fears over to Him, acknowledging that He's with you and that He will comfort you in the midst of your difficult circumstances.

DAILY SCRIPTURES

DAY 1
Psalm 23

DAY 2
Psalm 13:1-6

DAY 3
John 14:27

DAY 4
Philippians 4:4-8

DAY 5
1 John 4:18

YOU PLANNED EVIL AGAINST ME; GOD PLANNED IT FOR GOOD TO BRING ABOUT THE PRESENT RESULT—THE SURVIVAL OF MANY PEOPLE.

GENESIS 50:20

DEEPER LOOK

Now that you've honestly confronted the brutal facts about the fears you face and the consequences they bring about in your life, it's time to look at what God's Word has to say about facing your fears. The Bible is full of people who struggled with some of the same fearful circumstances you face.

Joseph was a man of God, yet he endured his share of difficulties and dangers. At one point in his story, Joseph was in an Egyptian prison, having been unjustly accused by his boss's wife (see Gen. 39:7-20). As you'll see, Joseph was given an opportunity to be set free from his wrongful imprisonment.

READ GENESIS 40.

Imagine that you're Joseph at the end of the events in this chapter. What would you think and feel in verse 23?

After all Joseph had been through in his life so far, what do you think kept him from giving up? (See 39:21 for at least one idea.)

Think of a situation you've been in that's comparable to Joseph's—when you were treated unfairly, for example, or when you were simply in a figurative dungeon because of your circumstances. Perhaps you prayed, asking God for just this one thing: that you'd feel better, that the relationship would be restored, that you'd get the job, that you'd find someone to love, or whatever that one thing was for you. But you didn't get an immediate answer. You were stuck where you were with no visible hope for a change in the situation.

Briefly describe that situation and the way it felt to you at the time.

How did you respond to God during that time?

At the end of Genesis 40, Joseph was in prison, having interpreted the dreams of his two cellmates, who'd been released. Joseph was hoping their releases would give him the opportunity to get out of the dungeon himself, but the chief baker was put to death, and the chief cupbearer returned to his position as Pharaoh's servant and forgot all about Joseph and his ability to interpret dreams. One day the chief cupbearer overhead Pharaoh telling his magicians and wise men about a couple of odd, troubling dreams he'd had, but the Egyptian experts couldn't interpret them (see 41:8). Suddenly the cupbearer had a flashback: "There was this guy I was in prison with who was great at interpreting dreams. In fact, he's the reason I'm your cupbearer again today. Oops, sorry I forgot about him. My fault."

They gave Joseph a quick shave and bath, threw some new clothes on him, and brought him to the palace, where he accurately interpreted Pharaoh's dreams.

When you read the whole story of Joseph's life (see 37–50), it's not hard to see God at work. In this particular story God used all the circumstances, even the ones that seemed bad at the time, to bring Joseph to a place where God could use him in extraordinary ways. If the cupbearer had remembered Joseph two years earlier, Joseph may not have been readily available to be called in to interpret Pharaoh's dreams. If the cupbearer hadn't remembered Joseph at this particular time, none of this would have happened. God is in charge of all the circumstances in our lives.

Turn back to Genesis 40:8; 41:16 and highlight Joseph's responses. What do these verses tell you about Joseph's character?

READ GENESIS 41:28-45.

Joseph went beyond what he was asked to do: interpret a dream. He actually advised Pharaoh, providing a 14-year plan for the kingdom. What gave Joseph such boldness to tell Pharaoh what he should do?

Joseph's faith and trust in God were finally rewarded. But remember that his clarity came only in hindsight. During those two years of waiting, Joseph kept his eyes on God, not on the seeming hopelessness of his situation. He didn't run ahead of God but waited for God's blessings.

How have you seen people, perhaps yourself, possibly miss out on God's blessings by not waiting for Him during difficult life circumstances? Think of a difficult marriage or job situation, for instance.

What have you learned from Joseph about keeping your focus on God rather than on your circumstances and your fears during a trying situation, even during a long time of waiting?

We've defined *fear* as *a heightened sense of vulnerability and a diminished sense of power.* Like Joseph, when you focus on God rather than your fears, you find confidence in trusting that He's in control.

When you trust God, do you feel more or less vulnerable? Why?

I can focus my attention on my problems, I can focus my attention on my fear, or I can focus on God.

When you stay focused on God, do you feel more or less in control over situations? How does your relationship with God change your need for control?

It's one thing to wait a couple weeks or months for God to respond in our painful circumstances; it's another thing to wait years as Joseph did. King David was also familiar with waiting for God to work on his behalf during dire situations.

READ PSALM 6:3; 13:1-4.

What was the one thing David asked God for in these passages?

What was David feeling as he called out to God? Record the emotional words you see in these verses.

What do you think about the brutally honest way David talked to God? Does praying to our holy, sovereign Lord in that manner seem disrespectful to you? Why or why not?

When you read other psalms by David and the historical books about his life, it's clear that he had the utmost respect and rightful awe for Almighty God (see Ps. 96:1-10 for one example). At the same time, David had a personal relationship with God that allowed, even demanded, total honesty. David knew he could pour out his real thoughts and undisguised feelings to God because he knew Him and trusted Him. We can't hide our true thoughts and feelings from God anyway, so why try to camouflage them when we pray?

READ PSALM 13:5-6.

In your Bible underline or highlight the first word *(but)* in verse 5. Why is that word significant?

Circle the action words in these two verses. Despite David's strong feelings in the midst of his troubles, how did he decide to respond?

What gave David the ability to trust, rejoice, and sing in his pain?

What do you learn about a relationship with God as you see people like Joseph and David deal with long-term struggles in their lives?

Close your Bible-study time with prayer. Use David's prayer in Psalm 13:1-6 as a template for your own prayer. Begin by simply telling God how you feel about the circumstance you're going through. Then use the word but *to make a transition, turning your focus to God and His faithfulness, His faithful love, and His generosity to you.*

COMPLETE CLARITY COMES ONLY IN RETROSPECT AND EVEN THEN ONLY AFTER TRUSTING GOD FOR ALL WE CAN'T SEE.

NOW WHAT?

So far you've evaluated your fears and the consequences of those fears in your life. You've studied the Bible to see examples of ways God's people responded to paralyzing fear. Now it's time to apply those biblical patterns to the way you live each day.

READ PSALM 121.

Highlight the words used to describe God in this passage.

Now use those words to complete the following sentences.

God, You are my ...

And You are my ...

Thank You for being my ...

What specific promises in this passage can you take hold of?

What does it mean to lift your eyes (see v. 1)?

From what are you lifting your eyes? What fear or false source of security has held your attention?

What will you do to lift your eyes and keep them focused on God?

Psalm 121 is one of 15 psalms collected as songs of ascents, which Jewish pilgrims sang as they traveled, or ascended, to Jerusalem to celebrate seasonal feasts. The journey had its share of dangers and hardships along steep and winding roadways. These songs reminded the people to look beyond their current circumstances to God, who was their Protector. Unfaithful Jews worshiped false gods in shrines in the high places on the hills, so this song also reminded the faithful to look beyond those idols to the one true God, the Maker of heaven and earth.

To lift our eyes today means to shift our focus from our own fears and circumstances, as well from as the idols of this world that we sometimes look to for security. As the apostle Paul wrote:

> We do not focus on what is seen, but on what is unseen.
> For what is seen is temporary, but what is unseen is eternal.
> **2 CORINTHIANS 4:18**

Psalm 121 reminds us to look up from our fears and circumstances to God, our eternal Creator and Protector.

How do we do that? It takes practice—spiritual practice. Those who are most successful at staying focused on God in the midst of troubles are those who spend time with God daily, reading His Word and talking with Him in prayer.

How will you practice lifting your eyes to God?

Our ultimate source of help is the Lord. He works through other people in our lives. He works in the midst of our circumstances and the fears that threaten to paralyze us. He's always working, providing help even when we can't see it at the time.

Even Jesus' disciples had to learn to lift their eyes beyond their current circumstances. They faced many fears as they walked with Jesus for three years. At times they seemed to be learning the lesson as they watched Jesus display His awesome power over disease, nature, and even death. But then the next minute they'd face a storm and once again be gripped with fear. Their experience probably sounds familiar to many Christians walking with Jesus today.

Shortly after Jesus' resurrection the disciples were hiding out together when Jesus walked in to change their perspective for good.

READ JOHN 20:19-22.

What fears were the disciples experiencing?

Where did their help come from?

What did Jesus do to calm their fears?

> Peace I leave with you. My peace I give to you. I do not give to you as the world gives. Your heart must not be troubled or fearful.
>
> John 14:27

Of course, the source of the disciples' fears didn't disappear; the religious leaders who'd killed Jesus were still around. But after this encounter with their risen Lord, the disciples stepped out of those fears and courageously stepped into the risky adventure of spreading the gospel.

What made the difference in their lives?

As you end your study time, use John 20:19-22 to compose your own prayer. Think again about your greatest fear and its consequences in your life. Ask Jesus to step into the room where you are now and into the middle of that fear. Hear Him say to you, "Peace to you!" (vv. 19,21). In prayer respond to His offer of peace.

WEEK TWO

COURAGE TO TRUST

START

At the end of group session 1, we were encouraged to watch for situations during the week when we might focus attention on our fears rather than on God.

- Did you notice a particular area where you were most prone to be afraid?

- What happened when you remembered Jesus' words not to fear and to take heart?

- What insights did you learn about fear, about yourself, or about God as you completed your personal study of week 1?

In session 1 we saw that the presence of fear isn't the problem; a lack of faith is. Learning to trust God is the keystone on which everything else rests. But what is trust? And how can we trust a God we can't see?

In the video for this session, Pete focuses on a person in the Bible whose life exemplifies trust: Joshua. We'll look to him as an example of how we too can live in such as way that our faith is bigger than our fears.

WATCH

Use the space below to follow along and take notes as you watch video session 2.

What fuels fear is when I take my eyes off God's love for me.

Depending on God isn't the absence of strength but the presence of courage.

It's on the other side of fear that freedom lies.

You are inwardly fashioned for faith, not for fear.

Scriptures: Psalm 121; Numbers 13:27,30-33; Exodus 33:8-11; Joshua 1:5; 3; 4:4-9; Deuteronomy 31:6,8

RESPOND

Use the statements and questions below to discuss the video.

Like Pete, many of us have probably seen God's faithfulness in the past, but for some reason we forget about it and clutch something in life we feel is secure.

When have you allowed fear to paralyze you? What were the circumstances? How did you view God's faithfulness at that time?

What do you think are the biggest barriers to letting go of your perceived control and putting your trust in God?

Discuss the following ways Pete described trust. How would you explain each, or how have you experienced each to be true?

Depending on God isn't the absence of strength but the presence of courage.

Trust isn't primarily a state of mind or the ability to think positive.

Trust isn't a blind leap into the unknown but the opposite. It ultimately depends on the type of knowledge that comes only with long acquaintance and intimate understanding.

There are two prevalent worldviews of what it means to trust. In the first we're in control of our own destiny. In the second God is in control; He's the only one we can ultimately trust.

Let's work together to create a one-sentence definition of *trust* that we can use over the next five weeks. How would you define *trust?*

Read aloud Joshua 1:1-9. What themes are evident in these verses?

Joshua is a great biblical example of what it means to trust God. When others were afraid, Joshua's trust in God propelled him forward; he knew the people could certainly do what others thought was impossible.

What do you think gave Joshua that kind of trust in God?

Joshua was ready to finally lead the people across the river and into the promised land. But there was a problem: the Jordan River was at flood stage. At this point the crossing of the Jordan must have looked like a bad idea to the Israelites. Clearly, the people didn't have the resources they needed to overcome the obstacle to their quest.

If you'd been in that crowd that day, what would you have said to the person next to you?

What fears would have risen up in you?

In the video Pete used the illustration of rock climbing to describe living our lives and growing in our relationship with God; many people have given up on progress and have settled for not falling. He mentioned that some things in life we tend to hold on to, things that feel safe to us, are merely illusions of control. Consider how you've experienced that reality in your life.

What motivates you to trust those things more than God?

What would you be giving up if you decided to let them go?

What fear would you need to step into?

What would you gain in the long run?

Each day between now and the next group session, identify times when you sense that you're settling for just not falling or, like the Israelites, staying in the desert you know rather than going into an unknown promised land. Think about the things you tend to hold on to tightly as objects of your control.

Complete the personal study for week 2 before the next group experience.

TAKING YOUR EYES OFF GOD'S LOVE FUELS FEAR.

PERSONAL REFLECTION

To begin moving freely in the direction God has for you, it's often helpful to first con-sider where you are currently. This was a regular practice of King David as he wrote his psalms. Often for David, the reality of his outward circumstances was evident; he spent much of his time during several stages of his life hiding in cold, dark caves or other places far from his palatial home in Jerusalem. But he also looked inside himself at the condition of his heart. Psalm 61 is one such reflection:

> God, hear my cry;
> pay attention to my prayer.
> I call to You from the ends of the earth
> when my heart is without strength.
> Lead me to a rock that is high above me,
> for You have been a refuge for me,
> a strong tower in the face of the enemy.
> I will live in Your tent forever
> and take refuge under the shelter of Your wings.
> **PSALM 61:1-4**

Take a moment to think about your present life circumstances. Choose a location to represent your circumstances, such as a cave (hiding), a ditch (stuck), an elevator (up and down), or a ski lift (moving upward). Then explain why you chose that location.

David asked God to lead him to a rock high above him. David's picture of God as a refuge, a strong tower, shows us why he trusted God so much. God's faithfulness and protection in the past allowed David to trust God in the present and the future.

Think about your current level of trust in God. Be honest with yourself about the way you'd describe it, not what you want it to be. What kind of refuge would best describe your trust in Him?

   Lord, You're my ...

Why did you choose this type of refuge? What does it represent about your trust in God?

David desired not only to visit God's sanctuary—that is, the place where God was present—but also to live there forever (see v. 4). The fellowship he had with God was so sweet that he didn't want it to end.

Consider ways you currently spend time with God, whether that means going to a corporate worship service on the weekend or spending time alone with God daily.

On the thermometer choose the temperature that best reflects your desire to spend time with God.

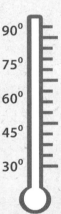

90°   Hot/passionate/on fire for God

75°   Warm/affectionate toward God

60°   Lukewarm/halfhearted

45°   Chilly/aloof toward God

30°   Frosty/coldhearted toward God

Why did you assign yourself that temperature? What do you think causes you to be in that climate of the heart?

Passion and presence are related. Spending time with God and trusting Him go hand-in-hand. The psalmists often wrote about God's presence and the hope it brought them.

What does each of the following verses reveal to you about your heart for God?

> You reveal the path of life to me;
> in Your presence is abundant joy;
> in Your right hand are eternal pleasures.
> **PSALM 16:11**

> I will see Your face in righteousness;
> when I awake, I will be satisfied with Your presence.
> **PSALM 17:15**

As for me, God's presence is my good.
I have made the Lord GOD my refuge,
so I can tell about all You do.
PSALM 73:28

May my prayer reach Your presence;
listen to my cry.
PSALM 88:2

You have set [my] unjust
    ways before You,
[my] secret sins in the
    light of Your presence.
PSALM 90:8

Where can I go to escape Your Spirit?
Where can I flee from Your presence?
PSALM 139:7

*Choose one verse from the previous list that
most accurately reflects your relationship
with God or that you desire to be true for you.
Write it on a separate piece of paper or index
card or email it to yourself. Read it several
times during the day to remind yourself of
God's presence with you. Memorize it so that it
becomes internal to your thinking and is set in
your heart. Close your time in God's presence
by talking to Him as you would converse with
a friend.*

DAILY SCRIPTURES

DAY 1
Psalm 61:1-4

DAY 2
Joshua 1:1-9

DAY 3
Joshua 4

DAY 4
Psalm 121

DAY 5
2 Timothy 1:7

HAVEN'T I COMMANDED YOU: BE STRONG AND COURAGEOUS? DO NOT BE AFRAID OR DISCOURAGED, FOR THE Lord YOUR GOD IS WITH YOU WHEREVER YOU GO.

JOSHUA 1:9

DEEPER LOOK

You've evaluated your level of trust in God and its connection to the time you spend with Him. Now you'll look deeper into God's Word to learn more about biblical trust.

First we need to see the foundation of trust. As we discussed in the group session, it took courage for Joshua to trust God in incredibly dangerous situations. When others lacked the courage to enter the promised land—when others saw giants—Joshua and Caleb saw a God bigger and stronger than any person or any other obstacle before them. The two men of God said, "We can certainly take the land." Why?

READ EXODUS 33:7-11.

Joshua may seem like a footnote in this story, but the significance of this scene is huge. Moses and Joshua had a specific place where they met with God: the tent of meeting (and later the tabernacle).

What does this passage reveal about Joshua's formative experiences before leading God's people on incredible adventures of faith?

Where is your tent of meeting—a specific place where you like to meet with God face-to-face?

Moses talked to God as two friends talk to each other. Joshua witnessed this close relationship. What's the connection between relationship and trust?

Joshua illustrates how we can develop stronger trust in God—a belief that God is all-powerful and ready to do something big through us if we trust Him. The Israelites' journey through the desert sounds like a Hollywood movie plot. The heroes escape and go on a long, eventful journey. It's one narrow escape after another, always just in the nick of time. Finally, they get to their destination, but a huge obstacle is in the way. They'll either give up or courageously go forward into battle. These adventure movies always end with the decision to go forward, despite the unlikely odds for success.

When we come to Numbers 13 in the Israelites' journey, the people were looking across the river at the land that God had promised to them since the time of Abraham (see Gen. 12:7; 13:15). At least twice the Lord plainly told the Israelites that He had "set the land" before them and that they should go and take possession of it (Deut. 1:8,21). The long-awaited promise was about to come true. All they had to do was to take action.

The Israelites sent 12 men—including Joshua—to scout out the situation. Forty days later the spies returned to Moses and the people with their findings.

READ NUMBERS 13:26–14:10.

Record the details of the scouts' report in the columns below.

                  GOOD NEWS   **BAD NEWS**

How would you describe the spies' point of view?

What words would you use to describe the perspective of the Israelite people (see 14:1-4)?

Time and time again on their journey to the promised land, God had allowed the people to come face-to-face with this fear of the unknown, and it paralyzed them. Their fears set limits on their lives. The Israelites had seen God provide for them in miraculous ways many times, yet each time their fears were stronger than their faith.

This incident wasn't the first time the Israelites wanted to go back to Egypt, where they'd been slaves for four hundred years. It was a constant refrain along their journey (see Ex. 14:11-12; 16:3; 17:3). They would have rather settled for the predictable patterns of their past than faithfully move forward into the future.

Fear imposes itself in the darkness and spins off all kinds of worst-case scenarios. The spies, as well as most of the Israelite people, dealt with a host of "What if?" impulses.

> Fear will set limits on your life, but it's on the other side of fear that freedom lies.

List as many "What if?" statements as you can find in Numbers 13:26–14:10, even if the words "What if?" aren't there.

Look again at Numbers 14:5-9 and compare the responses of these leaders to the reactions of the rest of the Israelites. In what ways did these leaders show trust in God in the midst of a fearful situation?

Moses and Aaron:

Joshua and Caleb:

What was their focus in comparison to the rest of the people?

The Israelites' fear of the unknown paralyzed them and discouraged them from taking what God wanted to graciously give them, so they wandered through the wilderness for a generation. Of the people who'd left Egypt 40 years before, all except Caleb and Joshua died before the Israelites finally had another opportunity to take possession of the land.

In Joshua 1 the new generation was undergoing a major transition after the death of their leader, Moses, as God prepared them to follow a new leader, Joshua, into the promised land. Between the Israelites and their promised territory flowed a raging, muddy torrent, and they weren't carrying rafts or canoes with them. How could an entire nation—women, children, supplies, and livestock, not to mention warriors with all their gear—possibly hope to get across this natural barrier and still be able to move and fight when they reached the other side?

READ JOSHUA 3.

What differences exist between this account and the previous time the Israelites had this opportunity to cross into the promised land (see Num. 13–14)?

What enabled Joshua, the priests, the 12 selected men, and the rest of the people to move forward as they approached and then walked into the Jordan River bed?

When God tells us to move out and watch what He's getting ready to do, we'd better start walking and looking. That's what Joshua did. He grabbed hold of the desire that God had planted in his heart, and he began moving forward, expecting God to make a way. He anticipated confirmation of his obedience to the destiny God had planned for him and his people.

Close your Bible-study time with prayer. First listen to God's words to you, the same words he spoke to Joshua:

> Haven't I commanded you: be strong and courageous? Do not be afraid or discouraged, for the LORD your God is with you wherever you go.
> **JOSHUA 1:9**

Read those words several times and let them sink in as you meditate on them. Then respond to God's encouragement to you. Be specific about the areas in your life where you need to be strong and courageous, trusting the Lord your God. Ask Him to help you take steps of faith into your "Jordan River," that raging torrent of fear in your life. Thank Him for His presence with you wherever you go.

YOU'RE INWARDLY FASHIONED FOR FAITH, NOT FOR FEAR.

NOW WHAT?

Now that you've evaluated your level of trust in God and studied the ways Joshua and the Israelites responded to God's leading, it's time to ask yourself, *Now what?* How will you apply these lessons to your life, especially to strongholds of fear?

In the group session we discussed the illustration of rock climbing. Try to imagine you're on a steep rock face one hundred feet above the ground. Because you have a good grip on some holds, you feel secure, but you've not yet reached the top of the climb. To move forward, you have to let go of your grip where you are so that you can reach up to the next hold, which is uncertain.

As you imagine this scenario in your mind, what words would you use to describe the way you feel?

What would it take for you to let go of that good grip, that control, in order to reach up? What might you need to remember?

In Joshua 4, as the last of the Israelites triumphantly stepped onto the banks of the Jordan, the Lord told Joshua to send 12 men, one from each tribe, back to the middle of the river, where the priests stood with the ark of the covenant. They were to pick up 12 stones from that place and carry them on their shoulders to Gilgal, where they would be camping. Joshua set up the 12 stones there as a monument; it would be a constant reminder of the day when God dried up the river and the Israelites crossed into the promised land.

In verse 23 Joshua referred to the crossing of the Red Sea (see Ex. 14). This event had happened 40 years earlier, before almost all the people crossing the Jordan were born. But surely the story had been retold over and over again through their years in the wilderness.

Imagine you were one of the people crossing the Jordan that day. In what ways would the stories of the Red Sea crossing have provided hope and trust as you and your friends crossed the Jordan?

Now imagine you were living in the promised land 10 or 20 years after this event and were facing a fearful situation. How would the monument in Gilgal or other monuments, such as the ruins of Jericho, have provided hope even in the midst of great danger?

Many times in the Old Testament at pivotal points in the history of God's people, the Israelites built altars or raised commemorative stones to remind them of God's great acts of deliverance. We can also create altars in our lives—tangible reminders of what God has done for us. By recalling ways God has worked in our past, we're better able to continually trust God for the future.

Our altars can consist of any number of physical reminders: a framed picture of yourself and the person who led you to Christ, the first dollar bill you received after you started your business, a ring your spouse gave you when you renewed your vows, a letter from a friend that encouraged you during a difficult time, a picture of your child that you keep on your desk or in your wallet, or a Bible verse that helped you through a dark valley in your life.

What's one altar you have, a tangible reminder of God's work in your life that strengthens your faith?

Take out this object and reflect on what it means to you. What thoughts or feelings does this object evoke in you?

Take a few moments to think about a way God has recently provided for you or come through for you. It may have been something big, such as the resurrection of a dying marriage or the healing of someone with cancer or another disease. Or it may be something relatively small but nonetheless significant for you. If you have difficulty thinking of something that's directly affected you, consider a way God has recently provided for a friend or a family member.

Take time to think about this event. Try to remember what you were thinking and feeling at the time. Then try to connect an object or a location to this memory of God's act of deliverance, healing, or provision. If you have an object small enough, hold it in your hands and let it remind you of God's faithfulness in your life.

If a specific location is connected to this event, consider taking pictures of that place to post on your walls, keep in your wallet, or use for the background or screensaver on your computer or another electronic device.

If you're creative, use your imagination and complete a project that reminds you of God's goodness and faithfulness. For example, you could draw a picture, write a poem or a story, or make a quilt.

What altar have you identified as a memorial to God's faithfulness?

Why is this object a significant reminder of God's activity in your past?

How does this altar provide hope for facing your fears in the present or future?

With this object in your hands or in mind, compose a worshipful psalm or prayer to God. For an example see Psalm 8, which King David wrote after looking into the night sky to consider God's power and worship Him as Creator. Spend time recalling God's faithfulness, as symbolized by the altar you've chosen. Worship God as your Provider, Protector, Healer, and Savior.

WEEK THREE
EMBRACING THE UNKNOWN

START

In the previous group session we were encouraged to watch this week for areas in our lives where we're stuck because we're clinging to something other than God.

- What did you notice since our previous group session about what motivates you to trust these objects or people more than God?

- From your personal study of week 2, would you be willing to share any altars you identified—physical reminders of what God has done for you in the past? How did that exercise help you trust God more for the future?

In this session we'll investigate what it will take for us to find courage to follow the passion God has placed in our hearts. We'll look at Daniel as the model of someone who embraced uncertainty and believed in the provision, promises, and power of God. Let's see what Pete has to say to us about embracing this adventure.

WATCH

Use the space below to follow along and take notes as you watch video session 3.

Fear sets limits for your life.

Peace isn't the absence of trouble; it's the presence of Christ.

Our journey of faith is a one-step-at-a-time process.

Trust that allows us to embrace uncertainty:

1. Belief in the provision of God

2. Belief in the promises of God

3. Belief in the power of God

The more spiritually mature you are, the less certainty you require.

Scriptures: Daniel 6:3-5,10,16-17,19-23; Acts 4:1-20; 27:13-26; Psalm 121:2-3

RESPOND

Use the following statements and questions to discuss the video.

In what area of life do you feel the most uncertainty?

Pete talked about big questions most, if not all, of us have. Some of the examples he mentioned were:

- When am I going to get married?

- When is my marriage going to get better?

- Will I ever find a job I love?

- Will I ever find freedom from this addictive cycle of sin?

- When will my prodigal child come to his or her senses?

- Will I be cured of this disease?

Let's each start by identifying our one big question. You may have more than one, but choose just one to share now.

What do you think would be a first step in trusting God with your big question?

How can this group help you take that step, embrace uncertainty, and trust God?

Toward the beginning of the video, Pete said it may sound harsh, but many of us have chosen, consciously or unconsciously, to stay in the predictable patterns of our past, no matter how painful those patterns might be, rather than venture into the unknown, where we have to trust the God we can't see.

On a scale of 1 to 5, with 1 being totally false and 5 being totally true, how accurate do you think that statement is for most people you know? Why?

Pete said that there's no such thing as a trouble-free life and that peace isn't the absence of trouble; it's the presence of Christ. If we lived with that principle firmly rooted in our lives, how would it help us embrace uncertainty and live the life of adventure God has for us?

A couple of phrases in Daniel 6 reveal Daniel's integrity, practices, and priorities. For example, when the jealous government officials were trying to frame him, the Bible says:

> They could find no charge or corruption, for he was trustworthy,
> and no negligence or corruption was found in him.
> **DANIEL 6:4**

Later, King Darius twice used a telling phrase: "your God, whom you serve continually" (vv. 16,20).

How would you describe Daniel's character?

How would you describe his walk with God?

In what ways did Daniel "live the life that leads to the answer," as Pete said in the video?

What's the role of consistency in living a life of trust in God?

We've mentioned the fact that clarity comes only with hindsight. As Pete said in the video, some of us might be paralyzed right now because we're not sure what steps await us. Like Indiana Jones, we may not be able to see the path and might need to take a step of faith to see that path materialize.

This week watch for ways you, with God's help, can embrace the uncertainty of taking your next step to trust God more, even without being able to see all the way to the end. Also consider how our group can help you take the next step, perhaps even a leap of faith, in trusting God more. Let's pray for one another that we can each trust God in an area of our lives that absolutely scares us to death!

Complete the personal study for week 3 before the next group experience.

PEACE ISN'T THE ABSENCE OF TROUBLE; IT'S THE PRESENCE OF CHRIST.

PERSONAL REFLECTION

We must begin this week's time of personal reflection by recognizing the folly of playing it safe by doing nothing at all to face our fears. Yet as we've seen, our fears can paralyze us; they can keep us from moving forward even though we know we need to take the next step.

King Solomon wrote:

> One who watches the wind will not sow,
> and the one who looks at the clouds will not reap.
> **ECCLESIASTES 11:4**

This verse simply says if we wait for the perfect conditions, we'll never act. We might think we're playing it safe, but we discover there's no safety in doing nothing.

List four or five areas of your life in which you've played it safe in the past by waiting for everything to be perfect before taking action.

Circle the one area you think has had the biggest impact on you.

Looking back on the situation now, what did you learn from it?

How have you viewed moving forward in faith? Be honest. Choose the more accurate response or record your own.

☐ Like rolling the dice: "There's no such thing as a sure thing, so I might as well try and see what happens."
☐ Releasing my attempts at security and grasping God's hand: "I know the future will always be uncertain, but I also know God is faithful no matter what the future holds."
☐ Other:

What does your response tell you about the way you view faith? God? Your relationship with God?

Mark your level of trust on the following scale.

1	2	3	4	5
I never trust anyone.			I'm completely trusting.	

Why do you think you evaluated your level of trust as you did? Does your assessment come from good or poor modeling by people you respected? From people who were trustworthy or untrustworthy in your past? From healthy relationships or hurtful relationships in the past?

Trust is the foundation of any relationship—your marriage, business, parenting, or small group, for instance. How have you seen your general level of trust affect your relationships?

Now consider your general level of trust and the way you arrived at that level. Describe the way your ability to trust has affected your relationship with God.

Take time to talk with God about your trust issues, whatever they are. If you've found it hard to trust others or God, tell Him so and turn over that hesitancy to Him. Ask Him for His power to help you trust Him more.

DAILY SCRIPTURES

DAY 1
Ecclesiastes 11:4

DAY 2
2 Corinthians 5:7

DAY 3
Daniel 6:10

DAY 4
1 John 4:4

DAY 5
Matthew 14:27-30

WE WALK BY FAITH, NOT BY SIGHT.

2 CORINTHIANS 5:7

DEEPER LOOK

Now that you've evaluated your tendency to play it safe and your level of trust, it's time to look at what God's Word has to say about these issues. Last week we studied one example of how the Israelites played it safe by sending spies into Canaan and then deciding to stay in the desert rather than cross into the land God had promised them (see Num. 13–14). The Bible is full of examples of people who decided to play it safe, as well as people who embraced uncertainty and lived a life of adventure. Five of these examples are listed in the chart below.

Read each Bible passage and fill in the chart by briefly answering the question for each person or group of people.

	Rich Man MATTHEW 19:16-22	Disciples MATTHEW 4:18-22	Jonah JONAH 1:1-3	Peter MATTHEW 26:69-75	Peter ACTS 4:1-13, 18-20
What uncertainties did they face?					
How did they respond—play it safe or trust?					
What did they gain?					
What did they lose?					

What do you learn from these examples about playing it safe versus facing uncertainties?

Look again at the last two passages about Peter. How do you explain the changes in Peter's attitude and faith between the time of Jesus' trial and the early days of the church?

Which of the people on the chart—the rich man, the disciples, Jonah, pretransformation Peter, or posttransformation Peter—do you relate to most? Why?

Moving away from an attitude of playing it safe requires going forward in the face of uncertainty. None of us ever get 100 percent clarity about the finish line while we're standing at the starting gate. Only by moving forward are we able to begin to see what might be next.

The group session introduced Daniel as an example of someone who exercised ordinary, day-to-day courage. Daniel's carefully formed habit of trusting God enabled him to do the next right thing and embrace uncertainty. In Daniel 6 some jealous government officials had a decree published that said anyone who prayed to a god or a person other than the king would be thrown in the lions' den. How would Daniel respond?

READ DANIEL 6:10.

What does the phrase "just as he had done before" tell you about Daniel's faith?

What does this passage tell you about the content of Daniel's prayer?

What does the content of Daniel's prayer tell you about his view of God and his attitude toward God?

How did Daniel's habit help him trust God rather than play it safe in the face of uncertainty and what probably looked like certain death to others?

Daniel's prayer life can teach us to embrace uncertainty, live by faith, and have a day-by-day relationship of obedient trust in God.

> The more spiritually mature you are, the less certainty you require.

Read the following prayers of Daniel. What does each prayer teach you in general about your relationship with God and your daily time of communing with Him?

   Daniel 2:20-23

   Daniel 9:4-19

What does Daniel teach you about these vital components of prayer?

Worship/praise:

Confession:

Repentance:

Supplication (asking God to work):

An effective prayer life is an essential part of building trust in our Heavenly Father. It's something we all desperately need yet often neglect. In fact, Christians often feel guiltier about their prayer habits—or lack of them—than almost any other aspect of their spiritual lives.

What keeps so many Christians from pursuing and maintaining a regular practice and discipline of prayer? Some people may say they don't have enough time, or other things in the world are putting pressure on them. Daniel faced deadly threats to his prayer life, yet he continued praying faithfully. For still other people, perhaps prayer is difficult because we pray to a God we can't see. Perhaps our prayer lives would improve if our eyes could be opened to see God.

READ 2 KINGS 6:8-17.

Imagine being this servant and discovering you're surrounded by a huge army that's there to capture you. What's the normal tendency of most people in that kind of circumstance?

What do you learn from this passage about the reality of spiritual forces we can't see? (If you'd like to get more insight into God's invisible angelic army, see Ps. 34:7; 125:2; Matt. 26:53; Eph. 6:12; Heb. 1:14; 11:27.)

What does 2 Kings 6:8-17 teach you about living by faith, not by sight (see 2 Cor. 5:7)?

You'll experience a breakthrough in your prayer life when you discover the freedom of praying whatever's on your mind and in your heart. That's when you'll begin to discover that every moment, every thought, every second is another opportunity to connect with your Father in heaven. Those moments become opportunities to build much-needed trust in God.

When you make time with God a continuous part of your daily life—when you learn to practice the presence of God, as the great monastic thinker Brother Lawrence taught—you'll find that the focus of your vision is continually being corrected. You'll begin to realize you're no longer surprised by conflict or adversity, because your trust in God has placed Him, rather than your situation, at the center of your life.

With your Bible still open to 2 Kings 6, end your Bible-study time with prayer. Ask God to open your eyes to His power, His provision, and His promises. Ask Him to help you understand that no matter what fear you're facing, no matter how great the odds that seem stacked against you, those who are with you far outnumber those who are against you.

YOUR JOURNEY OF FAITH IS A ONE-STEP-AT-A-TIME PROCESS.

NOW WHAT?

Studying the lives of biblical people can help you understand what it looks like to live a risky lifestyle of faith in pursuing God-given dreams, but of course, you still need to apply their examples to your own life. Certainly, learning to live a life of adventure by faith will require much of you. Embracing uncertainty means no more playing it safe. It means trusting a God you can't see. It means encountering stress, uncertainty, cost, discomfort, and a certain amount of temporary chaos. It requires you to learn new skills and acquire new relationships. None of these processes are without risk.

What potential costs, discomforts, or requirements keep you playing it safe instead of risking it all for God-given dreams?

What would living a life of adventure by faith require from you? What might need to change for you to embrace that adventure?

Where will you get the strength to take your next step to live this adventure of faith? Consider what you need from God; what you need to invest in your relationship with God; what you need from others, including your group; and what you need to invest in your group members.

In the video during the group session, trusting God one step at a time was compared to using a GPS app. We have to learn to trust the app to give us the next turn. But many of us spend so much time wanting to know the end of the journey that we never get to the beginning step. Of course, God is much more dependable than a GPS app, but this illustration may help you consider one important obstacle many people face in embracing uncertainty one step at a time: the need to be in control.

When you use a GPS app, how do you tend to use it (or how would you use it have you had one)? Select the response that best fits you.

- ☐ I enter my destination and trust the app one step at a time. I don't look ahead.
- ☐ I try to see the next several upcoming turns, just to be sure.
- ☐ I continually fidget with the app, checking what turns are coming up and how many miles, how much time, and how many turns are left.
- ☐ I don't really trust the app. I usually wonder whether there's a better alternative route to the destination.

What does your answer indicate about your need to be in control?

When it comes to control over your life, how well or poorly do you handle the idea that God is the captain of the ship, not you, and that His way is the best way? Why do you think you respond that way?

People who walk with God every day don't worry much about God's purpose for their lives. They're too busy trusting God one step at a time, doing the next right thing, to worry much about the result. They know the destination is in God's hands.

READ AGAIN DANIEL 6:10.

If you were arrested and accused of praying to God, what evidence would there be to convict you?

Of course, we can pray anytime and anywhere—commuting to work, pushing a cart through the grocery store, or sitting in the office. But we also need times of focused, dedicated prayer. We need to periodically set ourselves apart with no distractions—Jesus called it going into our "closet" (Matt. 6:6, KJV)—in order to pour out our hearts to God and carefully listen in our spirits for His answers.

How important do you consider having a specific time set aside for prayer each day?

How does (or how would) having a specific time for prayer help you build a stronger discipline of spending time with God?

How vital is it for you to have a specific place for prayer?

Close your study time with prayer. Ask God to show you what next step He wants you to take in carrying out the plans He has for your life. Ask Him to give you something God-sized—something so big that if He isn't in it, it's destined to fail. You can't do this in your own power. Then simply listen for Him to respond. Remember that God will respond according to His timing and in His way, not yours, so be patient and receptive. When you sense God showing you the next step, record it here.

WAITING ROOMS

START

Welcome to session 4 of *What Keeps You Up at Night?* Last week
we talked about embracing uncertainty and taking steps of faith.

- In what ways have you learned to trust God more, even when you can't
  see the destination to which He's leading you?

- What did you learn about playing it safe versus embracing uncertainty
  as you completed your personal study of week 3?

So far in this Bible study we've talked a lot about embracing uncertainty
and trusting God. But what do we do if we're trying to trust God in a
very uncertain, difficult situation, constantly praying for an answer, but
no answer comes? What do we do while we wait for God to answer,
to work, to supply? Pete has answers to our questions about waiting.

WATCH

Use the space below to follow along and take notes as you watch video session 4.

Benefits of waiting:

1. Refines our character

2. Brings spiritual transformation

3. Teaches us to hope patiently and place our trust in God and His schedule

It's on the other side of the dark valley that we see the most growth and the most fruit.

Act on the belief that God has a plan and that He's bringing it to completion in your life.

Scriptures: Isaiah 40:31; Psalm 23:4; Luke 2:25-38; Acts 1:4-8;
John 11:3,5-7,14-15,21-22,39-45

RESPOND

Use the statements and questions below to discuss the video.

Let's start with Pete's questions.

> When have you been in the waiting room of life—when all you could do was wait? How did you feel, and what did you do while waiting?
>
> Why do you think waiting is so difficult for most of us?

Pete identified three benefits of waiting:

1. Waiting can be a crucible for refining our character.

2. Spiritual transformation happens while we're waiting, not when we get what we want.

3. Waiting can give us a long-range perspective as we hope patiently and place our trust in God and His schedule.

> What example of one of these benefits can you give from your life?

Mary and Martha are biblical examples of people who were in the waiting room of life.

> Imagine you were Mary or Martha and your brother got sick and died. What would keep you up at night as you went through this trial?
>
> When you asked Jesus to come and He didn't show up, what emotions do you think you would have felt? Why?

Like other people in the Bible we've studied, Mary and Martha received clarity only in hindsight. Yet they had faith in Jesus along the way.

> What does having faith look like in your life—not yet knowing what will happen but trusting God regardless of the outcome?

Jesus lived by God's calendar throughout His life, and He consistently tried to teach His disciples to live by that timetable. In this account they learned the lesson by seeing firsthand the result of waiting. Later, when Jesus washed their feet, He said to Peter:

> What I'm doing you don't understand now, but afterward you will know.
> **JOHN 13:7**

> Why was it so important for the disciples to learn to live by God's timetable before Jesus physically left this world?

Often a time of waiting corresponds to a "dip" in our lives.[1] For some time the graph of our lives moved up and to the right, but then that growth slowed or stopped, and we felt as though we were in a dark valley. We've probably all had that experience at some point in our lives. Pete said it's often during this dip that people give up—on their marriages, on their ministries, on themselves, on their faith. But it's on the other side of that dip that we see the most spiritual growth and fruit.

> Describe a dip in your life that you experienced.

> How did it feel at the time? What were you thinking?

> How did you get through it?

> What happened on the other side?

This week take some time to think about things you're still waiting for: health, work, love, a resurrected relationship, the return of a loved one, Christ's return, and so on. Consider ways you can make the most of that time of waiting.

Complete the personal study for week 4 before the next group experience.

1. Seth Godin, *The Dip: A Little Book That Teaches You When to Quit (and When to Stick)* (New York: Penguin, 2007).

JUST BECAUSE A DREAM IS DELAYED DOESN'T MEAN IT'S DENIED.

PERSONAL REFLECTION

As you begin this time of reflection and personal evaluation, it's vital to recognize that we sometimes change and grow the most during times of waiting and struggling.

Take a few moments to think about the span of your life: highs; lows; times of growth; and emotional, psychological, relational, and spiritual plateaus. After you've taken a few moments to reflect on your life in these areas, draw a simple line graph of your lifetime in the space below. Include two or three highs, such as meeting your spouse, getting married, having kids, becoming a Christian, and so forth. Also include two or three lows, such as losing a job, getting separated or divorced, the death of a loved one, and so forth. You might also consider times of stagnation when you just drifted along.

What's the highest of highs on your graph? Write a one- or two-sentence prayer thanking God for that mountaintop.

What's your lowest low on the graph, a dip in your life that felt like "the valley of the shadow of death" (Ps. 23:4, KJV) at that time?

How did you get through that dip? Select the most appropriate responses. You can choose more than one.

☐ I don't know. I just muddled along, and then life got better.
☐ I leaned on a couple of good friends. I wouldn't have gotten through it without them.
☐ I depended on God. He walked through the valley with me and saw me through it.
☐ A church was very helpful to me.
☐ A pastor, counselor, psychiatrist, or doctor helped me and directed me to the resources I needed.
☐ Other:

How did you feel when you were in the dip?

How does it feel now as you look back on it?

Over the past three sessions we've looked at three Bible heroes: Joseph, Joshua, and Daniel. Each of these men had to wait on God for something and for some time, often many years. Joseph's waiting room was a prison, where he faithfully prayed and waited for his chance for deliverance. Joshua's waiting room was the desert; he waited for decades to enter the promised land that he knew was the destiny of his people. For Daniel it was Babylon, a waiting room he would apparently never leave, and yet God used him in incredible ways in that place.

Waiting is a common activity for those who passionately follow God. That's not all bad, by the way. Sometimes it's when we're at our lowest and weakest that we realize how high and powerful our God is.

What waiting room are you in right now?

How would you assess the way you're handling your wait? In each pair of words below, circle the word that best describes how you're doing.

Patient   Impatient

Active   Passive

Peaceful   Worried

Content   Fearful

How does your relationship with God affect the way you handle times of waiting in your life?

READ PSALM 119:81.

Close this personal-reflection time in prayer, honestly sharing with God how you feel about the lows in your life and any time of waiting you're experiencing now. Turn over your waiting room to Him by simply putting your hope in Him.

DAILY SCRIPTURES

DAY 1
Psalm 119:81

DAY 2
Isaiah 40:31

DAY 3
Acts 1:7-8

DAY 4
John 11:1-45

DAY 5
John 16:33

THOSE WHO WAIT ON THE Lord SHALL RENEW THEIR STRENGTH; THEY SHALL MOUNT UP WITH WINGS LIKE EAGLES, THEY SHALL RUN AND NOT BE WEARY, THEY SHALL WALK AND NOT FAINT.
ISAIAH 40:31, NKJV

DEEPER LOOK

Now that you've reflected on and evaluated the ups and downs in your life, especially the way you deal with dips and times of waiting, it's the perfect time to look at what God's Word has to say about times of waiting for God to take you to the next step in His plan for your life.

As we discussed in our previous group session, Mary, Martha, and Lazarus went through a huge dip in their lives when Lazarus got sick and then died. While Jesus could see how this episode in their lives would end, his friends, including the disciples, had no idea. They had to wait and see. And of course, only Jesus knew how long the wait would be. We have a lot in common with Mary, Martha, and Jesus' apostles.

READ JOHN 11:1-7,17-37.

How would you describe the relationship between Jesus and this family (Lazarus, Mary, and Martha)? How did Jesus feel about them? How did they feel about Him?

What sense do you have of Jesus' control over the situation throughout the passage?

What were Jesus' main concerns throughout the narrative?

How would you describe Mary's and Martha's responses during this situation? Choose any that seem true.

- ☐ Wide mood swings
- ☐ So emotionally distraught that they really didn't know what they were saying or thinking
- ☐ Anger at Jesus
- ☐ Anger at God
- ☐ Serious doubting
- ☐ Incredible faith

Do Mary's and Martha's reactions seem like normal ways to respond in such a situation? Why or why not?

READ JOHN 11:38-44.

How do you assess Martha's initial reaction to Jesus' plan? Was it a lack of faith or a dose of reality? Why?

We don't know exactly what happened between verses 44 and 45, but it would be interesting to see Mary's and Martha's reactions to this miracle.

A couple of days after all this happened, as the two sisters sat down and talked about it, how do you think they would have understood all the circumstances? What lessons would they have learned?

At the center of our struggle with waiting is the conflict between our timeline and God's. Because we're limited by our perspective as time-bound creatures, we'll never be able to grasp the vast difference between the way we view the events in our lives and the way God views them. This is where faith and trust must enter.

Mary, Martha, and countless others would tell you from their experiences that life's waiting rooms are difficult places, even for people with great faith and trust in God. But they might also tell you in hindsight that it's often when we're at our lowest and weakest that we realize how high and powerful our God is. Paul certainly realized this. In 2 Corinthians 12 he related his struggle with "a thorn in the flesh" (v. 7)— the particular, intimate vulnerability that vexed him most deeply.

READ 2 CORINTHIANS 12:7-10.

What purpose for his struggle and waiting did Paul identify?

Grace can be defined as *God's provision for our every need when we need it.* How does that definition help you make sense of struggles and times of long waiting?

A literal interpretation of verse 9b is "My power is being perfected in your weakness." In other words, God's provision of grace is a continuing process, not a one-time event.

How does that interpretation help you understand how God is working in the midst of troubles or times of waiting?

In what ways was God's answer to Paul's prayer better than what Paul was actually praying for?

What does this passage teach you about prayer?

What does it teach you about troubles and waiting?

What does it teach you about God and your relationship with Him?

> When our trust is in the Maker of heaven and earth, we realize that what matters most isn't what's happening *to* us but what's happening *in* us.

We don't get to see God at His most powerful unless we spend time in the waiting room. When we're highly aware of our own inadequacy, that's when we need to be most aware of God's unlimited ability. When we face unpleasant, fear-inducing circumstances, we must face them with faith in the God who's watching over our lives. Sometimes the best thing we can do is nothing; we just wait.

Read the following Bible verses and underline words or phrases that are commands for you to obey. Then circle each promise and provision God's Word gives to those who wait on Him.

Those who wait on the LORD
Shall renew their strength;
They shall mount up with wings like eagles,
They shall run and not be weary,
They shall walk and not faint.
ISAIAH 40:31, NKJV

I am certain that I will see the LORD's goodness
in the land of the living.
Wait for the LORD;
be strong and courageous.
Wait for the LORD.
PSALM 27:13-14

We wait for Yahweh;
He is our help and shield.
For our hearts rejoice in Him
because we trust in His holy name.
PSALM 33:20-21

LORD, I wait for you;
   you will answer, Lord my God.
PSALM 38:15, NIV

I waited patiently for the LORD,
and He turned to me and heard my cry for help.
He brought me up from a desolate pit,
out of the muddy clay,
and set my feet on a rock,
making my steps secure.
He put a new song in my mouth,
a hymn of praise to our God.
PSALM 40:1-3

What do these verses teach you about ways God responds to people when they wait for Him?

Close your Bible-study time by using Psalm 40:1-3 to guide you in prayer. Turn each He *into* You *as you speak the words of these verses to God. Personalize the verses as much as you want to fit your circumstances. Start your prayer like this:*

> I have waited patiently for You, Lord,
> and You turned to me and heard my cry for help.

KEEP DOING THE NEXT RIGHT THING.

NOW WHAT?

Now it's time to apply your evaluation and study times to the real-world situations of your life in which you're waiting and wondering what to do next.

Recall the account of Jesus, Lazarus, Mary, and Martha. Describe a time when you went through something similar to Mary and Martha— when you asked Jesus to come and fix something, and you trusted Him to do so, but He didn't seem to show up. You waited and waited, but you saw things go from bad to worse. Record your story.

Looking back at that time, do you see things differently now than you did then? If so, how?

What have you learned from that experience?

Take Paul's statement in 2 Corinthians 12:10, "When I am weak, then I am strong," and reword it in a more specific, personal way for a situation you have faced or are facing.

When I am weak; that is, when ... (describe the situation when you feel weak):

then I am strong because ... (describe what God does in the circumstance: how he provides His grace, His power, and His transformation):

Jesus commissioned his followers: "Go ... and make disciples of all nations" (Matt. 28:19). "Go into all the world and preach the gospel to the whole creation" (Mark 16:15). But before they were to go, Jesus told them to stay and wait.

READ ACTS 1:4-8.

Some of the apostles, especially their leader, Peter, tended toward action. Peter was impetuous. Two other apostles were called "Sons of Thunder" (Mark 3:17); that doesn't sound like guys who were very patient.

If you were one of those disciples, what would have been going through your mind and heart after you heard Jesus' commission but were then told to wait?

Why was it vital for the disciples to wait?

In what area of your life are you waiting for God's "green light" (for example, a life decision, a change in careers, a ministry to get involved in)?

Jesus told His followers, "It is not for you to know times or periods that the Father has set by His own authority" (Acts 1:7). What does that statement imply for your time of waiting?

Based on what you've learned in this lesson, how will you actively wait on God, even for His timing with the dreams He's given to you?

The Christian life is full of periods when we must wait for God's timing to fulfill His promises. God's people waited centuries for the coming of the Messiah. People like Simeon and Anna (see Luke 2:25-38) waited their entire lives for this Child to be born, the Child who would redeem God's people. Today we're actively waiting for Jesus to return (see Matt. 24:14) and to take us to our true home in heaven. Although we don't know when He will return (see v. 36), we're to wait and stay prepared (see vv. 42,44).

READ MATTHEW 24:42,44; TITUS 2:11-13.

What are we called to do as we wait for Jesus' return?

How does waiting for Jesus' future return put your present waiting into perspective?

Keep Titus 2 open in front of you and close your study time with prayer. Ask God to give you a bigger perspective on waiting, on time, and on His calendar as you live in this present age. Ask Him for His grace and power as you go through your day and as you patiently wait for His perfect timing in the fulfillment of all His promises.

HOLY RHYTHMS

START

In the previous group session we talked about the importance of waiting on God's timetable. In this session we'll talk about what we can do while we wait.

- What did you notice since the previous session about making the most of waiting?

- What did you discover in your personal study this week about waiting, trusting, or growing?

So what do we do while we're waiting? Does faithful waiting mean we passively stick our hands up in the air until God rains blessings down into our palms? On the contrary, waiting involves actively seeking God. As we'll see in this week's video, such a pursuit may involve a recalibration of our lives.

WATCH

Use the space below to follow along and take notes as you watch video session 5.

Most of the time we really don't have a fear problem; we have a trust problem.

We can purposefully, proactively discipline ourselves to recognize God's presence.

1. The discipline of Sabbath

2. The discipline of prayer

3. The discipline of reading God's Word

Spiritual disciplines are meant to be a way of life.

Scriptures: Galatians 5:25; Genesis 3:8; Matthew 6:6; Psalm 13:1-3,5-6; John 15:4-5

RESPOND

Use the statements and questions below to discuss the video.

Who would like to start by sharing a way you've recently connected with God, such as prayer or Bible reading?

On a scale of 1 to 10, how connected to God do you feel right now?

1	2	3	4	5	6	7	8	9	10
Nowhere close						Overwhelmed by His presence			

Pete told the story of God's calling him to plant a church. God was showing Pete that He would prompt him to do some things that wouldn't make sense to other people and that might scare Pete to death. Pete learned that the objective isn't to fear less. It's to trust God more, to keep God, not self or anything else, at the center of the story.

Have you ever had an experience in which God called you to do something that perhaps other people didn't understand or that scared you to death? What did you do? What did you learn from it?

Because we tend to measure ourselves against the wrong standards—other people, for instance—rather than God, we regularly need to recalibrate or realign our lives with the right standard. That standard is our Creator.

What most often causes us to get out of calibration or misaligned in our relationship with God?

What are the effects of being out of calibration or misaligned in your life?

Pete described Adam and Eve walking with God in the garden of Eden. Before the fall the couple was perfectly aligned with God and had an intimate relationship with Him. The story of the Bible is about God's reaching out to us. He sent prophets to call us back to Him. He sent Jesus into the world so that we could have a relationship with Him. Our God desires to spend time with us. If we stay in close fellowship, we're ready to hear His voice when He directs us to take the next step in His plans for our lives.

What keeps Christ followers from spending time with God?

In John 15 Jesus described our relationship with Him as branches to a vine. We must remain in Him, "the true vine" (v. 1), to bear fruit in and through our lives.

What practices and disciplines most effectively enable and encourage you to spend time with God and get in sync with His voice, His activity, and His will?

What's your biggest obstacle to spending more time with God daily?

If you're not in sync with your Creator, you'll chase your own dreams instead of His perfect will. As you complete your personal study this week, try to discover spiritual practices that help you stay connected to God. Experiment with spiritual disciplines you haven't used before. Then share what you're doing and encourage other group members through phone calls, texts, emails, or social media. At our next session we'll share our experiences with one another.

Complete the personal study for week 5 before the next group experience.

THE QUESTION ISN'T WHETHER GOD WANTS TO BE WITH YOU. INSTEAD, THE QUESTION IS, DO YOU WANT TO BE WITH HIM?

PERSONAL REFLECTION

Remember that most of the time, we don't really have a fear problem; we have a trust problem. That's a fundamental truth to grasp as we begin to assess our relationship with God. We need to clearly see our relationship with God in order to clearly see areas in which we're living in fear instead of living in faith. Until we trust Him, we'll never be able to fully experience all He has for us.

Take a moment and consider one of your deepest fears. To what extent is that issue related to your trust or lack of trust in God?

What would it look like to trust God more and surrender that fear to Him?

We've said from the beginning that the object of this study isn't learning to fear less; it's learning to trust God more. It's moving our fears and ourselves out of the center of the story and placing God there—back in His rightful place as the central focus of our lives. This may mean we need to discover or rediscover how to walk with God since we easily get out of step and sidetracked in our day-to-day lives.

How would you assess your current relationship with God? Select the most accurate response. You may choose more than one if necessary.

☐ I'm walking a couple steps behind Him; I'm a follower, but I'm staying at a safe distance.
☐ I'm walking in the opposite direction.
☐ I often find myself running ahead of Him.
☐ He's very distant right now; I'm not sure where He is or how to connect with Him.
☐ I was trying to walk with Him, but I feel as if He deserted me.
☐ I've walked with Him, but I got distracted or lost along the way.
☐ He's reaching out to me; I need to grab His hand and go with Him.
☐ We're walking side by side, and I'm loving it.
☐ He's carrying me.

Explain your answer. Why did you choose the response(s) you did? How did you get to that point?

How would you describe your level of satisfaction with your current walk with God?

Think for a moment about all that's implied by taking a walk with someone. Obviously, we don't take a walk with a concept or a theory. We take a walk with a person. The very act implies a relationship.

READ PHILIPPIANS 3:12-14.

What do you learn from Paul about discipline and your journey with God?

To close your personal-reflection time, select the Scripture below that's most relevant to you and your situation. Use it to begin your prayer as you spend time talking with God.

You reveal the path of life to me;
in Your presence is abundant joy;
in Your right hand are eternal pleasures.
PSALM 16:11

Even though I walk through
   the darkest valley,
I will fear no evil,
   for you are with me;
your rod and your staff,
   they comfort me.
PSALM 23:4, NIV

You, LORD, rescued me from death,
my eyes from tears,
my feet from stumbling.
I will walk before the LORD
   in the land of the living.
PSALM 116:8-9

DAILY SCRIPTURES

DAY 1
Philippians 3:12-14

DAY 2
Matthew 11:28

DAY 3
Ephesians 3:14-21

DAY 4
John 15:1-8

DAY 5
Galatians 5:25

COME TO ME, ALL OF YOU WHO ARE WEARY AND BURDENED, AND I WILL GIVE YOU REST.

MATTHEW 11:28

DEEPER LOOK

Now that we've reflected on our relationship with God, it's vital to investigate His Word to discover ways we can stay connected with Him.

Because we live in an imperfect world, we tend to drift away from God. Our relationship with Him gets out of sync, so we need to spiritually recalibrate on a regular basis. But against what or whom will we measure our lives? Friends? Coworkers? Other Christians?

Read the following verses and circle words or phrases that indicate what's of first importance in our lives as Christians.

> Fear of the LORD is the foundation of true wisdom.
> All who obey his commandments will grow in wisdom.
> Praise him forever!
> **PSALM 111:10, NLT**

> Jesus replied, " 'You must love the LORD your God with all your heart, all your soul, and all your mind.' This is the first and greatest commandment. A second is equally important: 'Love your neighbor as yourself.' The entire law and all the demands of the prophets are based on these two commandments."
> **MATTHEW 22:37-40, NLT**

What do these passages identify as the standard by whom or what we're to measure ourselves?

God created us in His own image, so our truest identity is found only in Him. "Fear of the Lord" (Ps. 111:10) means giving Him the reverence He deserves as our all-powerful, almighty, everlasting Creator and King. By giving Him reverence, we acknowledge His rightful place as the Lord of our lives.

How does putting God in His rightful place help us measure ourselves against the right standard?

How does making our love for God the primary focus help us live in proper alignment with Him?

READ JOHN 15:1-8.

Name specific resources the Vine (Jesus) supplies to the branches (us) that we need to live, grow, and bear fruit.

What are some ways we can remain in Him?

What are the results of remaining in Jesus?

What are the consequences of not remaining in Him?

What does Jesus promise to people who stay connected to Him?

The people who are most successful in staying aligned with God's purpose are those who've consciously built seasons of spiritual discipline into their lives, not as a way to earn God's favor or to get God to love them more. God already loves you more than you could possibly imagine, and there's nothing you can do or fail to do that will change His love for you. Rather, the purpose of spiritual disciplines is to provide intentional opportunities to listen to God, align your heart and mind with Him, and discern and follow His will.

READ 1 TIMOTHY 4:7B-8.

Think of areas in your life for which you've trained, such as athletics, education, work, or ministry. What goes into a training regimen? What do you have to sacrifice?

Why do people engage in physical training? What's the point?

Why should you train yourself in godliness?

READ 1 CORINTHIANS 9:24-27.

What's the goal of discipline, self-sacrifice, and hard work for a Christ follower?

One definition of *discipline* is *to train yourself to do something by controlling your behavior*. In what ways must you control your behavior when practicing spiritual disciplines?

The most important thing you can do as a Christian is to stay connected to Jesus. That's your number one priority.

Even when we don't view spiritual disciplines as religious merit badges, we sometimes think of them as obligations— chores we do to remain in good standing with God. However, if we see them for what they really are, we realize they're actually opportunities. God is inviting us to experience and enjoy His holy presence. Spiritual practices such as prayer, Scripture, and contemplation attune us to the holy rhythm of God's movement in our lives. Only by aligning our hearts with Him can we remain in His will as we pursue the plans He's given us.

Read the following passages and answer these questions about each one: What spiritual discipline(s) do you see? What are the spiritual benefits of that discipline?

EXODUS 20:8-11

PSALM 119:97-98

MATTHEW 6:1-4

MATTHEW 6:5-13

MATTHEW 6:16-18

HEBREWS 10:24-25

1 JOHN 1:9

Which of these disciplines have you used to grow closer to God? Place a check mark beside each one.

Which disciplines have you never tried? Circle them.

As you read each of the passages above, were there any spiritual disciplines you felt God leading you to engage in? Which one(s)?

When we look at our modern culture, we realize how little we seem to value quiet and solitude. In our ever-expanding demand for more choices and more on-demand services, almost everything today is available 24/7. You can go to the grocery store at three in the morning; you can drown out the stillness of the night with an endless selection of cable-TV channels or streaming video.

But this isn't how we were meant to live. At the very beginning, when God created the universe, the Bible says He did all His work in six days, and on the seventh day He rested. For that reason the Sabbath is a day of rest and contemplation. It's another way we honor the divine spark in us, recalibrating ourselves to the standard of the One who made us in His image. We need regular times of quiet, rest, solitude, and reflection. We need to build Sabbath into our lives because this is how God wired us. When we ignore this needed rest, we get out of calibration with our Creator.

What does the fact that God set aside one day of the week as the Sabbath indicate about the nature of humankind?

What does God's institution of Sabbath reveal about Him and His attitude toward the people He created?

What do these passages indicate about what's of first importance in our lives?

To develop a deep, lasting trust in God, you have to spend time with Him. You have to spend time reading His Word and conversing with Him in prayer. You can't skimp on your time with God and still pursue a life of faith.

Maybe in this study you've identified a passion or dream God has called you to pursue. If you want to pursue His plan with confidence and purpose, you have to find ways to stay connected with Jesus, day to day and moment to moment.

One of the best ways to do develop intimacy with Christ is to spend time in prayer. An effective prayer life is an essential means of building trust with our Heavenly Father.

To close your Bible-study time, read Matthew 11:28-30. Take time to reflect on this passage and to consider what God is saying to you today. Listen to Jesus invite you into a refreshing relationship with Him, not into religious routine. Take time to rest in Him, to rest even from speaking words to Him in prayer. Simply be still and know that He is God (see Ps. 46:10, KJV).

CONSCIOUSLY BUILD IN SEASONS OF SPIRITUAL DISCIPLINE IN ORDER TO REALIGN WITH GOD'S DREAM FOR YOUR LIFE.

NOW WHAT?

So far this week you've reflected on your need to spend time with God. The next vital step is to make some decisions about what changes, commitments, or recommitments you'll make in your life in order to chase the dreams He's invited you to pursue.

What areas of weakness do you sense in your walk with God? Consider, for example, a lack of understanding of God's Word, impatience, pride, busyness, or ongoing sin.

Is there a particular discipline that would help you in your area of weakness? If so, what is it?

Remember that spiritual disciplines are meant to enhance and cultivate your relationship with God. It's not about the practices themselves. Everyone is different, so the way someone else practices a spiritual discipline may not necessarily work for you. If a spiritual practice isn't leading you to the Father's heart, it may not really be a spiritual practice for you; it may have become a religious ritual.

Think about the spiritual disciplines you've practiced in the past and currently practice. Have any become empty rituals for you? If so, how have they failed to bring you into a true connection with God?

What spiritual practices have been meaningful in your relationship with God?

What will you do to change the way you're approaching this spiritual discipline, or what new spiritual discipline will you try?

Sometimes spiritual disciplines have different value for us in different parts of our journeys. A practice that was beneficial to you in your walk with God when you were a less mature Christian may not be as beneficial to you today. Consider the spiritual disciplines—or the way you're approaching them—that at one time helped you grow in your faith but are no longer making an impact on you. For example, some people have found that reading through the Bible in a year was beneficial for them at one time, but now it's more helpful to read, study, and meditate on smaller sections of Scripture, one chapter, or even just a few verses each day.

Think about your need for Sabbath rest and ways it might help you pursue God. It's vital that you don't wear yourself out, even in the pursuit of God-given dreams. Determine now to take some time out each week, perhaps on a specific day or at a specific time of day, to come to Jesus and allow Him to give you the rest you need.

Record your plan for Sabbath by answering the following questions.

What day and/or times will you set aside? Put them on your calendar.

What will you do (or not do) during this time (for example, prayer, Bible study, meditation, solitude, or fasting)?

Some people find that designating a specific place for their time with God helps them focus. Where do you plan to spend this time?

Do you need to tell someone else about your plans and ask them to hold you accountable? If so, whom?

Other plans and details:

Read the following prayers from the Bible and respond to each one by answering these questions: How would you describe the hearts of the people who were praying? What did they pray for? How can you apply their prayers to your own prayer life?

PSALM 139

JOHN 17:13-23

ACTS 4:23-31

EPHESIANS 3:14-21

Close your study time with prayer. Choose one of the previous prayers and read it one more time, this time making it your own prayer. Speak it to God, changing any words as needed to make this prayer personal. Ask Him to refresh and empower you by His Spirit, keeping you in sync with the holy rhythm of His will for your life.

WEEK SIX

LIVING
YOUR
ADVENTURE

START

Welcome to our final session of *What Keeps You Up at Night?* In the previous group session we were encouraged to experiment with new forms of spiritual practices in order to discover ways to draw closer to God each day.

- Did anyone try a new spiritual practice that brought you closer to God?

- What did you discover about personal spiritual practices or about your relationship with God through your personal study this week?

Throughout this study we've talked about the imperative of making sure God is at the center of our focus. He—not our dreams and not our fears—is the central character in our stories. To live in that reality, we must surrender certain things, and as Pete tells us in our video today, it's by surrendering that we find our greatest adventures.

WATCH

Use the space below to follow along and take notes as you watch video session 6.

It may be that the thing keeping you up at night is actually not fear but passion.

For those who begin following their passion, fear is almost always replaced by a sense of calling.

Control is a myth.

Surrendering to God's desire for our lives means we choose to align ourselves with His greater purpose.

God's will is about who you become.

Scriptures: John 10:10; Genesis 12:1-5; 15:4-5; 22:1-19; Hebrews 11:8; Luke 10:27; 22:42

RESPOND

Use the statements and questions below to discuss the video.

As Pete mentioned, surrender may not currently feel natural to many of us, but a life of surrender should become a normal lifestyle for us as Christ followers.

What's one thing you sense God might want you to surrender?

What struck you most from Pete's story about his first trip to India?

Pete briefly talked about the challenges he and others faced on this trip. What kinds of fears do you think he and others faced as they moved forward?

Pete said, "Your adventure is connected to your passion, to how God created you." How have you seen that to be true in your life?

Pete identified three important principles in regard to our passions and dreams:

1. Fear defeats more dreams than all other causes combined.

2. The thing keeping you up at night may not be fear but passion; it may be the dream God has given you to fulfill.

3. Control is a myth.

Which of these principles rings true for you? Why?

Consider this definition of *surrender: letting go of something in order to take hold of something infinitely better.* How does this definition change the way you've understood surrender?

At the end of Genesis 11 and the beginning of Genesis 12, we're introduced
to Abraham (called Abram at this time). The Bible says:

> The LORD said to Abram:
> > Go out from your land,
> > your relatives,
> > and your father's house
> > to the land that I will show you.
> > I will make you into a great nation,
> > I will bless you,
> > I will make your name great,
> > and you will be a blessing.
> > **GENESIS 12:1-2**

What was Abraham surrendering?

What costs were involved for Abraham to do what God was calling
him to do? What were the benefits?

Pete talked about a "container" each of us has called "My Life"—an image of what we
believe our lives will look like. It holds all our hopes, dreams, and objectives that define
the direction we intend for our lives to take.

Think about different periods in your life. How has your container
changed over time?

How would you describe the shape of your container today?

In what ways has this study put something new into your container,
taken something out of your container, or changed the shape of your
container? What's your greatest lesson from this study of fear and faith?

Let's close this session by praying that we'll keep our hearts open to the possibility that
our containers for the future may not look exactly like what we've imagined them to
be. Let's pray for one another that we'll live with passion instead of fear, embracing
an attitude of "Not My will, but Yours, be done" (Luke 22:42).

Video sessions available for purchase
at *www.lifeway.com/upatnight*

GIVE GOD YOUR FEARS AND LIVE FOR ADVENTURE.

PERSONAL REFLECTION

To move from fear to freedom, from being stuck to chasing your dreams, you'll begin this time of reflection by considering your mental picture of what you want your life to be someday. In the group session this mental image of your life was described as a container holding all your goals, hopes, and dreams.

What does your container look like? Honestly describe what comes to your mind as you think about your hopes and plans for your life.

As you reflect on your life so far, has the shape of your container changed? If it has, how did you react? If it hasn't, how do you think you'd react if it changed?

How would you honestly assess your control over your life? Mark your rating on the scale below.

1	2	3	4	5	6	7	8	9	10

"I am the master of my fate,   God is sovereign in my life;
I am the captain of my soul."[1]   He's in total control.

What's your reason for this rating?

"Am I living God's will for my life?" is a question many Christians ask and some obsess about. It can feel complicated and overwhelming, but the answer is found simply in the way we respond to a handful of key Scriptures.

Read each of the following verses and select the applicable statement in each pair.

"Seek first the kingdom of God and His righteousness, and all these things will be provided for you" (Matt. 6:33).

☐ I'm seeking first the kingdom of God.
☐ I'm seeking my own kingdom first.

"This is God's will, your sanctification" (1 Thess. 4:3).

☐ The Holy Spirit is progressively conforming me to the image of Jesus Christ.
☐ I'm becoming more like the world around me each day.

"Rejoice always! Pray constantly. Give thanks in everything, for this is God's will for you in Christ Jesus" (1 Thess. 5:16-18).

☐ I'm living a life of joy even in the midst of troubles.
☐ I'm living a life of fear and worry.

☐ Through regular prayer I'm staying connected with God.
☐ My life is disconnected from God.

☐ I'm thankful to God.
☐ I'm ungrateful.

What do your responses indicate about whether you're living in God's will?

Several times during his life, Abraham surrendered his will to God. He said, in effect, "God, here's my container. Even though it holds all my desires for the future, I freely give it to You. I'll let You pour my dreams into a different container that You choose for me. And I'll trust You for the outcome."

Circle the word or words below that best describe how you feel about surrendering your container to God.

Nervous	Anxious	Scared	Angry
Sad	Suspicious	Overwhelmed	Uncontrolled
Ambivalent	Hesitant	Submissive	Secure
Confident	Trusting	Joyful	Empowered

Why did you choose the word(s) you did? What's going on in your heart as you consider surrendering control of your dreams to God?

Now imagine the new vision God wants to give you, a new way of looking at your life and dreams for your future. Go back to the list and draw a rectangle around the words that describe the way you feel about this new container.

How might your life change if you embraced this new vision?

READ PSALM 143:10.

David humbly admitted that he needed God to teach him to do His will. That's a great place to start as you close your time of reflection and personal evaluation. Ask God to teach you to do His will, surrender your container to Him, and allow Him to lead you into the great adventure He has for you.

1. William Ernest Henley, "Invictus" [online, cited 3 February 2015]. Available from the Internet: *www.poetryfoundation. org/poem/182194.*

DAILY SCRIPTURES

DAY 1
Psalm 143:10

DAY 2
Hebrews 11:1

DAY 3
Psalm 138

DAY 4
Matthew 6:25-33

DAY 5
John 10:10

NOW FAITH IS THE REALITY OF WHAT IS HOPED FOR, THE PROOF OF WHAT IS NOT SEEN.

HEBREWS 11:1

DEEPER LOOK

Now that you've evaluated your desires and expectations for life and your perspective on surrendering to God's will, it's vital to examine God's Word more deeply on this topic.

God's will isn't as complicated as Christians sometimes make it out to be. Usually, it's not so much about what you do, where you live, whom you date or marry, or where you work; it's more about who you're becoming. God's will is that we love God and love others (see Luke 10:27), and we can do that a lot of different ways.

READ PROVERBS 4:7; 16:22-23; 1 CORINTHIANS 10:31; COLOSSIANS 3:17,23.

What do these verses teach about God's will and human will?

What do these passages tell you about how God calls you to live?

We need to avoid paralyzing self-doubt that prompts us to agonize over simple decisions when God may be saying, "Either one is great. Just choose one and glorify Me with your choice." God gave you the ability to make decisions, and He gave you the guidance of His Word and His Holy Spirit for making decisions.

In the group session we discussed Abraham's life of faith and surrender. Throughout his life his faith was tested, and he passed. It might seem that once Abraham saw the birth of his son, which occurred in a way that was beyond anything he and his wife could have hoped for under normal circumstances, he would have been on cruise control from that point forward. After all, the man was one hundred years old! Surely by this point he was ready for a well-deserved retirement and no more surprises, right?

READ GENESIS 22:1-18.

How did Abraham feel about his son?

What do these verses suggest about Abraham's faith in God?

In the larger view of this narrative, God didn't want Abraham to kill his son. God had condemned human sacrifice (see Lev. 20:1-5). But God did want Abraham to surrender Isaac in his heart; He wanted Abraham to keep Him first in his life, loving God more than he loved anything else in the world, including God's gift of this promised son.

READ GENESIS 22:5,8 AND HEBREWS 11:19.

What do these verses suggest about trusting God regardless of the appearance of your circumstances?

Abraham's experience points forward to God's sending His Son—His only Son—into the world as our sacrificial Lamb to bring us back into a relationship with God. Even Jesus, in the great mystery of being fully God and fully human, willingly surrendered His desires to God's will for His life—and for His death. Jesus is our prime model of surrendering to God and living for His will. If we want to surrender to God's will, we'll live a Christlike life.

READ LUKE 22:39-44.

Describe Jesus' emotions as He prayed just before being arrested, falsely tried, and then crucified.

From a purely human standpoint, what was Jesus' desire?

How would you describe Jesus' passion and courage during this time?

What are the connections among fear, surrender, trust, prayer, and courage?

It isn't difficult to see the implications of Jesus' example for those who follow Him. As the ultimate hero, Jesus faced humanity's final and most intractable opponent— death—and emerged victorious. It was a harrowing experience, and it required of Jesus the most unwavering faith and the most undaunted courage the world has ever seen. Yet He faced the challenge and triumphed over it.

We can't tread any path that our hero hasn't already walked before us. There's no demon and no enemy—including death—we'll ever face on our journey that our hero hasn't already conquered. No matter what our quest is or where our adventure takes us, Jesus Christ has already gone ahead of us to show the way and to give us victory.

Jesus modeled a sacrificial life for His disciples, but He also constantly taught them with His words what surrender should look like in the life of a believer.

READ MATTHEW 5:11-12;
JOHN 15:18-19; 16:33.

What was Jesus' main message to His followers in these passages?

For what kinds of experiences was He preparing us?

What do these verses indicate about what's expected of a follower of Christ?

Surrendering to God means we choose to align ourselves and our purpose with His greater purpose. This type of surrender is the opposite of defeat. When we surrender to God, He gives us victory.

Of all the many promises Jesus gave us, safety is nowhere to be found. And when you think about it, how could it be any other way? Try to come up with a single great thing in the history of humankind that was accomplished entirely without risk. I'll save you some time; you can't.

READ LUKE 14:25-27.

How did Jesus define *discipleship?*

To live as a disciple of Jesus, what must we surrender?

Should we tell people about the costs of following Jesus before they make that decision? Why or why not?

Jesus used hyperbole in this passage to say, in effect, "Your love for Me must be greater than your love for your family." This was the same message God gave Abraham in Genesis 22 about his son Isaac. It's the same message Jesus communicated when He spoke about things in this world we tend to worry about:

> Seek first the kingdom of God and His righteousness,
> and all these things will be provided for you.
> MATTHEW 6:33

And it's the same message God gave in the First Commandment:

> I am the LORD your God. … Do not have other gods besides Me.
> **EXODUS 20:2-3**

God wants to be our first priority, and He wants us to trust Him for everything else. That requires surrender—sacrificing all those other things—even our plans and dreams for our lives.

READ ROMANS 12:1-3.

What does the image of "a living sacrifice" (v. 1) evoke in your mind?

How did Paul describe worship in this passage?

How does surrender help a believer discern "the good, pleasing, and perfect will of God" (v. 2)?

Close your Bible-study time by using Romans 12:1-3 as an outline for your prayer. Begin by presenting yourself to God as a living sacrifice, surrendering yourself to Him. Take time to worship Him. Ask Him to transform you by changing the way you think about your priorities and your plans for your life. Trust that His will for you is truly "good, pleasing, and perfect" (v. 2). Ask Him to direct your path toward the great adventure He's planned for you. Start by surrendering the rest of your day to Him.

SURRENDERING TO GOD'S DESIRE FOR OUR LIVES MEANS WE CHOOSE TO ALIGN OURSELVES WITH HIS GREATER PURPOSE.

NOW WHAT?

You've reflected on your dreams for your life and dug deep into God's Word to see what it teaches about surrendering your plans to God's will. Now it's time to decide whether and how you'll surrender to God and live a life of passion and adventure.

At the beginning of the group session, you were asked to share one thing God might want you to surrender. Now that you've had time to evaluate yourself more closely and study Scripture, try to flesh this out in more detail. Take a few moments and prayerfully reflect on what you sense God is calling you to surrender to Him right now. This may be a sinful pattern in your life, a bad habit, a plan or dream you have for the future, or anything or anyone you place above Him.

List 5 to 10 things you sense that you need to surrender to God.

Now prayerfully look over your list. Is there one item that stands out from all the rest as something God is asking you to release to Him? Circle it.

How will you take action to surrender this item to Him? What part will prayer, confession, repentance, Bible study, Bible memorization, fasting, and/or seeking others' help and encouragement play in this? Record your plan.

Giving up on our need to control our lives is a battle each of us will fight, in one form or another, every day we walk this earth. We keep forgetting that control—for humans, at least—is an illusion. Even when we think we have it, we really don't.

Instead of seeing this reality as negative, you can view it as positive. Instead of focusing on your lack of control, you can be thankful for the constant flow of new experiences, ideas, and opportunities that God brings into your life. Instead of pleading for your old container or demanding that God restore it to its original shape, you can accept with thanksgiving the one He's placing in your hands, trusting that it will do a better job of holding the future He's prepared for you.

Think about a plan you've made that you're currently pursuing. What if God interrupted your plan? Try to imagine that scenario. What would you do?

Sometimes we have to surrender our plans even in the midst of pursuing them. This doesn't mean we're giving up, just that we're handing over to God the responsibility for the outcome.

READ ACTS 15:36-41.

What did Paul and Barnabas surrender as they went their separate ways?

What did the kingdom of God gain?

Think about your group or church for a moment. What would you surrender if you or others stepped out in faith and started a new group?

Would you see this as negative or positive, an obstruction in your life or a new faith adventure? Why?

Letting go isn't the same thing as discarding. We don't know God's plans for the people, things, and events that have contributed to our lives. Just because they aren't part of our journey anymore doesn't mean God isn't using them for His purposes. Sometimes trusting God means accepting that our paths must diverge from the people, places, and things that have become familiar to us. As we let go and continue trusting, God enables us to continue our journey toward all He wants us to become.

As we learned earlier in this study, moving forward in a life of faith can be compared to rock climbing. To complete the climb, you must be willing to let go of one good hold to grasp another.

You've already considered what you need to let go of. What do you sense that God wants you to take hold of next?

List everything going on in the world that fuels your passion or provokes holy discontentment. Commit to bring these things to God in prayer each day for a month.

Before ending this study, review your responses to the activities you've completed over the past six weeks. List anything that stands out to you: lessons you've learned, areas in which you've grown, or perspectives that have changed.

READ PSALM 138.

Close your study time in prayer, thanking God for who He is, what He's doing in your life, and what He's doing to fulfill His purpose for you. You don't have to live in fear. Your unfulfilled desires don't have to keep you up at night as you restlessly toss and turn. God has created you for a great adventure of faith. It starts today. Your first step toward chasing your God-given dreams is surrendering any illusion of control and trusting that He's good. His plan for your life is greater than you could ever imagine.